Welcome to your mind

Whether you use this journal as part of your daily morning and evening routine or as a go-to tool when you're feeling called to write, fill these pages with all that is occupying your mind.

This journal is your new tool for healing, releasing, gaining clarity, creating, growing, feeling inspired, practicing gratitude, manifesting and so much more.

What you write doesn't have to make sense, it doesn't have to be spelled correctly and it doesn't have to be neat - it's simply a way for you to take what's in your mind and put it onto paper - so dive on in and find joy in the process!

Before each journaling session read the following affirmations. Believe them, embody them and watch your life transform:

I release what no longer serves me
I call in my wildest desires
I get to know myself at my purest level, my soul

For more support on your journaling journey head to https://thejournalclub.mykajabi.com/

Love and light,

Jess

DATE:

DATE:

DATE:

DATE:

Date:

DATE:

DATE:

DATE:

DATE:

DATE:

DATE:

DATE:

DATE:

Date:

DATE:

DATE:

DATE:

Date:

DATE:

DATE:

DATE:

DATE:

DATE:

DATE:

DATE:

DATE:

DATE:

DATE:

DATE:

DATE:

Date:

DATE:

DATE:

DATE:

DATE:

DATE:

Date:

DATE:

DATE:

Date:

DATE:

DATE:

DATE:

DATE:

DATE:

DATE:

DATE:

DATE:

Date:

DATE:

DATE:

DATE:

DATE:

DATE:

DATE:

DATE:

DATE:

DATE:

DATE:

DATE:

DATE:

DATE:

DATE:

DATE:

DATE:

DATE:

DATE:

Date:

DATE:

DATE:

DATE:

DATE:

DATE:

Date:

Date:

DATE:

DATE:

DATE:

DATE:

Date:

DATE:

DATE:

DATE:

DATE:

Date:

DATE:

DATE:

DATE:

DATE:

DATE:

DATE:

DATE:

DATE:

DATE:

DATE:

DATE:

DATE:

DATE:

Date:

DATE:

DATE:

DATE:

Date:

DATE:

DATE:

DATE:

DATE:

Date:

DATE:

DATE:

DATE:

Date:

DATE:

Date:

DATE:

Date:

DATE:

DATE:

DATE:

Date:

DATE:

DATE:

DATE:

Date:

DATE:

DATE:

DATE:

DATE:

DATE:

DATE:

DATE:

DATE:

DATE:

DATE:

DATE:

DATE:

DATE:

DATE:

DATE:

DATE:

Date:

DATE:

DATE:

Date:

Date:

Date:

DATE:

DATE:

Date:

Date:

Date:

DATE:

Date:

DATE:

DATE:

DATE:

DATE:

Date:

DATE:

DATE:

DATE:

Date:

DATE:

DATE:

Date:

DATE:

DATE:

DATE:

Date:

DATE:

DATE:

Date:

DATE:

DATE:

DATE:

DATE:

Date:

DATE:

DATE:

DATE:

DATE:

DATE:

DATE:

DATE:

DATE:

DATE:

Date:

DATE:

DATE:

DATE:

DATE:

DATE:

Date:

Date:

DATE:

DATE:

DATE:

Date:

DATE:

DATE:

DATE:

DATE:

Date:

DATE:

DATE:

DATE:

DATE:

DATE:

DATE:

DATE:

Date:

DATE:

DATE:

DATE:

DATE:

Date:

DATE:

DATE:

DATE:

DATE:

DATE:

Date:

DATE:

Date:

Date:

DATE:

Date:

DATE:

DATE:

DATE:

DATE:

DATE:

DATE:

DATE:

DATE:

DATE:

DATE:

DATE:

DATE:

DATE:

Date:

Date:

Date:

DATE:

DATE:

DATE:

DATE:

Date:

DATE:

DATE:

DATE:

DATE:

Date:

DATE:

DATE:

DATE:

DATE:

DATE:

Date:

DATE:

DATE:

DATE:

DATE:

DATE:

DATE:

DATE:

DATE:

DATE:

Date:

DATE:

DATE:

DATE:

DATE:

DATE:

DATE:

DATE:

DATE:

Date:

DATE:

DATE:

DATE:

DATE:

DATE:

DATE:

DATE:

DATE:

DATE:

DATE:

DATE:

DATE:

DATE:

DATE:

Date:

DATE:

DATE:

Date:

DATE:

Date:

DATE:

DATE:

DATE:

DATE:

DATE:

DATE:

DATE:

DATE:

Date:

Date:

DATE:

DATE:

DATE:

DATE:

DATE:

DATE:

DATE:

DATE:

Date:

Date:

DATE:

DATE:

DATE:

DATE:

Date:

DATE:

Date:

Date:

DATE:

DATE:

DATE:

DATE:

DATE:

DATE:

DATE:

DATE:

Date:

DATE:

Date:

DATE:

Date:

DATE:

DATE:

DATE:

DATE:

DATE:

Date:

DATE:

DATE:

DATE:

DATE:

Date:

Date:

DATE:

DATE:

DATE:

DATE:

DATE:

DATE:

DATE:

DATE:

DATE:

Date:

Printed in Great Britain
by Amazon